# THE LETTER FROM HEAVEN

## IT'S NOT WHAT YOU'VE IMAGINED

G. Albert Darst

D1527670

*The Letter from Heaven: It's Not What You Imagined*
Copyright © 2017 by G. Albert Darst
Paperback ISBN: 978-1-63073-206-6
Hard cover ISBN: 978-1-63073-218-9

Faithful Life Publishers & Printers
North Fort Myers, FL 33903

FaithfulLifePublishers.com
info@FaithfulLifePublishers.com
888.720.0950

Previous book by the author:
***The Revelation of Jesus Christ in the Old Testament***

20  19  18  17    1  2  3  4  5

*Presented To:*

_____

*From:*

_____

*On This Date & Year of Our Lord*

_____

# Dedication

*This book is dedicated first and foremost to the precious Saviour of all that will believe, the Lord Jesus Christ.*

*This book is also dedicated to Barbara, my wife of fifty years, who is now in the presence of her Lord and Saviour.*

# Acknowledgements

*To Pastor and Mrs. Bill Amberg*
*and*
*the members of Lighthouse Baptist Church*
*Fort Wayne, Indiana*
*who have made the publication of this book possible.*

*To Phil and Sharon Palinkas*
*for encouragement and proof reading.*

*To Jim and Una Wendorf*
*of Faithful Life Publishers*
*for their dedication and assistance.*

# Table of Contents

# The Weaver

My life is but a weaving
Between my Lord and me,
I cannot choose the colors
He worketh steadily.

Oft times He weaveth sorrow,
And I in foolish pride,
Forget He sees the upper
And I, the underside.

Not 'til the loom is silent
And the shuttles cease to fly,
Shall God unroll the canvas
And explain the reasons why.

The dark threads are as needful
In the Weaver's skillful hand,
As the threads of gold and silver
In the pattern He has planned.

— Grant Colfax Tullar

# Introduction

My wife of fifty years went home to be with the Lord Jesus Christ on April 29, 2016, after a 2 1/2 year battle with cancer. Though many suffer terribly, God spared my wife much (but not all) of the pain of cancer. During this time, Barb and I came to realize that the cancer was God's method (for her) of taking her home to Himself. You and I may walk a different road.

My wife took chemotherapy for two years, until infections brought that treatment to a halt. At the end, radiation was tried, but it was too little too late—Barb was too weak to endure it.

Barb was saved in July of 1976, at the age of 32, at the altar of a small independent Baptist church in Sarasota, Florida. A high school girlfriend had witnessed to her for many years. Although Barb was under conviction, it was not yet God's timing. Barb also listened to a well-known Baptist preacher on TV. Though she was often brought to tears, she was not brought to repentance and faith.

Because we put our boys in that Baptist church's Christian school, Barb attended (and then I attended) the church's services. The pastor was doctrinal and every message centered on salvation in Christ. I do not remember how many Lord's Days she held on to the pew in front of her while the invitation was given; but one Lord's Day the floodgates of conviction opened. She turned to me and said, "If you want to go to Hell, you will have to go alone." She went forward to make her calling and election sure. Sealed in Christ, she began the journey of her life, touching many hearts and souls along the way. Barbara was an example of a Proverbs 31 wife, mother, and woman. Many younger women called her *Mother Darst*.

Hopefully, you realize that Barb could not write a letter from Heaven. My intention with this *letter* is to dispel the many false perceptions associated with our journey to and sojourn in Heaven. Heaven is not what most of us have heard or think; i.e., just a happier place with the giddy sentimentality of earth. Heaven is what God has prepared, not what man has devised.

I am using this method, *The Letter from Heaven*, to encourage dear brothers and sisters in Christ, who are traveling the road to Heaven on the bus of affliction. Be assured that God's plan and purpose for *your life* is being worked out in the hands of a loving Father. You may not enjoy the trip, but stay focused on the destination. It will be worth it all when you see the Lord Jesus Christ!

— G. Albert Darst, 2017

**Explanation:**

The scenes depicted in this book relate only to those who died in Christ during the church age (The time-period from Christ's founding of His churches until the catching away/rapture of those in Christ). Once those in Heaven are reunited with their glorified earthly bodies and those on earth are caught away/raptured before dying, the saint's circumstances in Heaven change slightly because everyone then has a glorified body. These changes are outside the scope and reason for this volume.

Also, this is not a theological treatise on Heaven. This is a *scriptural picture* of what my wife is experiencing in Heaven. From what she experiences, and based on the Scripture references, you can formulate a biblical doctrine (teaching) of what Heaven is actually like.

# The Blessed Truth

*In the beginning—God* (Genesis 1:1).

On the sixth day of Creation;

*So God created* (from the dust of the ground) *man in His Own Image* (moral likeness)*, in the Image of God created He him; male and female created He them* (Genesis 1:27).

Thus, from the only eye-witness account ever placed upon the written record *[God is not a man, that He should lie;...* (Numbers 23:19)*]* mankind was created at the beginning by God. Therefore God, in His unique authority as Creator and Sovereign of the heavens and the earth, owns the created.

*For every house is builded by some man; but He that built all things is God* (Hebrews 3:4).

Further, the Creator fashions each human at conception. Every man/woman has proceeded from the originals—Adam and Eve.

*But now, O LORD, Thou art our Father; we are the clay, and Thou our Potter; and we all are the work of Thy hand* (Isaiah 64:8).

Further the Creator infuses each human, at conception, with the spirit of life.

*And the LORD God formed man of the dust of the ground, and breathed into his nostrils the breath of life; and man became a living soul* (Genesis 2:7).

Further, the Creator controls and directs the destiny of the created.

*A man's heart deviseth his way: but the LORD directeth his steps* (Proverbs 16:9).

*The steps of a good man are ordered by the LORD: and he delighteth in His way* (Psalm 37:23).

Further, the Creator grants to each human the number of his or her years.

*And the time drew nigh that Israel* (Jacob) *must die* (Genesis 47:29).

*The days of our age are threescore years and ten; and though men be so strong that they come to fourscore years: yet is their strength then but labour and sorrow; so soon passeth it away, and we are gone* (Psalm 90:10 from the Great Bible of 1539).

Thus God directs our destiny, while granting us a small circle of freedom in which to exercise our will. This then guarantees that in whatever state we find ourselves, it is the will of God. Think not that your present circumstances, though abhorrent and distasteful, are somehow outside the will of God. Whatever the state of your present life in Christ, this is the will of God for you.

> *In every thing give thanks: for this is the will of God in Christ Jesus concerning you* (1 Thessalonians 5:18).

Think not that your present circumstances are beyond the love of God. God *is* love and God's love *is* sacrificial love directed toward you. God loves you, not because of who you are, but because of who He is. Your circumstances do not change who God is. It is His love for you that is drawing you to Himself, despite your trials.

> *...Yea, I have loved thee with an everlasting love: therefore with lovingkindness have I drawn thee* (Jeremiah 31:3).

> *And we know that all things work together for good to them that love God, to them who are the called according to His purpose* (Romans 8:28).

> *And the Lord direct your hearts into the love of God, and into the patient waiting for Christ* (2 Thessalonians 3:5).

Think not that God's grace and mercy are no longer effective in your present circumstances. God's grace (which means that God is always disposed toward you) is just as active, and maybe more so, as He draws you ever upward to Himself. God's mercy (acts of grace) has made death the ultimate and permanent way of escape from the sorrows of this life for the believer.

> *And now, brethren, I commend you to God, and to the Word of His grace, which is able to build you up, and to give you an inheritance among all them which are sanctified* (Acts 20:32).

> *That as sin hath reigned unto death, even so might grace reign through righteousness unto eternal life by Jesus Christ our Lord* (Romans 5:21).

Then the question arises, "Is God responsible for your present circumstances?" It seems highly unlikely, but no man knows the mind of God. And even if a man knew the mind of God, no man can thwart the will of God. I can say for sure that sin (missing God's standard), Adam and Eve's original disobedience toward God, is the human cause of your present circumstances. All roads lead back to sin, and all sin leads back to the sin-nature of man. The sin-nature of man is the result of God's curse on man's disobedience in the Garden of Eden. (See Genesis 3:1-24.)

*Wherefore, as by one man* (Adam) *sin entered into the world, and death by sin; and so death passed upon all men, for that all have sinned* (Romans 5:12).

Another question arises, "Who is best able to determine the method by which a saint transitions or journeys to Heaven?" It is, after all, only a move from one location (earth) to a new location (Heaven). Is the Creator, who knows and is in control of every twist and turn of your journey, best able to determine which path is best for each of His creations? Or is the myopic saint, who knows nothing of the journey, best able to make the decisions as to what is best? The question answers itself!

*...when my heart is overwhelmed: lead me to the Rock that is higher than I* (Psalm 61:2).

The next question arises, "But why is there pain and discomfort?" Pain and discomfort are the mechanisms that God has installed in the human body as an indication that something is wrong. Pain and discomfort trigger a response in a person to look for relief. Pain and discomfort are also part of the *fall of man*. Because the human body lies under the Curse, the body is subject to many ailments—some of which God uses to take you to Himself.

*For we know that the whole creation groaneth and travaileth in pain together until now* (Romans 8:22).

*Wherefore let them that suffer according to the will of God, commit the keeping of their souls to Him in well doing, as unto a faithful Creator* (1 Peter 4:19).

The next question is, "But why do some folks linger at the edge of death for so long?" First, what appears to us to be *lingering* is actually the outworking of God's will for that person. Second, God still has a purpose in that person's life that He wants accomplished. Third, since the Creator determines the exact moment of someone's death, based on His own purpose and plan, the *time* has not yet arrived.

*Seeing his days are determined, the number of his months are with Thee, Thou hast appointed his bounds that he cannot pass* (Job 14:5).

*I Am He that liveth, and was dead; and, behold, I Am alive for evermore, Amen; and have the keys of hell and of death* (Revelation 1:18).

*For I reckon that the sufferings of this present time are not worthy to be compared with the glory which shall be revealed in us* (Romans 8:18).

For the lost, this *delay* is the longsuffering of God. It gives each person extra time, under adversity, to exercise *Repentance* (a change of mind) *toward God and faith* (trust) *toward our Lord Jesus Christ* (Acts 20:21).

> *For God so loved the world, that He gave His only begotten Son, that whosoever believeth in Him should not perish, but have everlasting life* (John 3:16).

For the saved, this *delay* is a further opportunity to exhibit Christ-likeness and bring glory to (to make known) God. Perhaps there is one lost person who needs to see how a suffering saint goes out into eternity. Even a non-responsive Christian can have a testimony for God to the lost and saved people that visit and care for the believer.

> *For to me to live is Christ, and to die is gain...For I am in a strait betwixt two, having a desire to depart, and to be with Christ; which is far better: nevertheless to abide in the flesh is more needful for you* (Philippians 1:21, 23, 24).

The next question is, "Why do I have to go this way?" Remember that Jesus said, *I Am the way* and so The Way has determined your way and the end of your ways. As there was a divine purpose in your birth, then in your life, so there is also a divine purpose in your death. Only the sovereign Creator knows His purpose in the manner of your home-going. It is our divine privilege to acknowledge and accept His wisdom, love, and compassion during the dark days of our lack of understanding. We live by faith in Him and we die by faith in Him.

*What time I am afraid, I will trust in Thee* (Psalm 56:3).

*For which cause we faint not; but though our outward man perish, yet the inward man is renewed day by day. For our light affliction, which is but for a moment, worketh for us a far more exceeding and eternal weight of glory; While we look not at the things which are seen, but at the things which are not seen: for the things which are seen are temporal; but the things which are not seen are eternal* (2 Corinthians 4:16-18).

Thou wilt not leave us in the dust:
Thou maddest man, he knows not why;
He thinks he was not made to die
And Thou hast made him: Thou art just.

(Tennyson)

The last question is, "Can you trust God with all the *unfinished* work of your life?" I remember my wife asking me in the waning days of her earthly existence, "Will you be all right?"

Just as I was part of the *unfinished work of her life*, so too are your loved ones that must be left behind in the care of their Creator. And He, who neither slumbers nor sleeps, will spread His wings to keep and protect those that you leave behind.

> *Trust in the LORD with all thine heart; and lean not unto thine own understanding* (Proverbs 3:5).

Brief life is here our portion,
Brief sorrow, short-lived care;
The life that knows no ending,
The tearless life is there.
(copied)

Therefore, we are left with the knowledge that God is the original Cause; God is the only Creator; and God is the eternal Sustainer. Because of who He is, we can trust in His Fatherly care to move us from this life of woe to a heavenly life of joy—and, at the same time, to watch over our loved ones that are left behind.

The runway may be rough.

> *There hath no temptation* (trial) *taken you but such as is common to man: but God is faithful, who will not suffer you to be tempted* (tried) *above that ye are able; but will with the temptation also make a way to escape* (the issue referring to the end of one's life)*, that ye may be able to bear* (endure) *it* (1 Corinthians 10:13).

But the landing will be smooth.

*But He knoweth the way that I take: when He hath tried me, I shall come forth as gold* (Job 23:10).

*But as it is written, Eye hath not seen, nor ear heard, neither have entered into the heart of man, the things which God hath prepared for them that love Him* (1 Corinthians 2:9).

*For we know that if our earthly house of this tabernacle were dissolved, we have a building of God, an house not made with hands, eternal in the heavens* (2 Corinthians 5:1).

*For here have we no continuing city, but we seek one to come* (Hebrews 13:14).

# God as Incomprehensible

*O the depth of the riches, both of the wisdom and knowledge of God! how unsearchable are His judgments, and His ways past finding out!* (Romans 11:33).

Since God is incomprehensible, and He is, then Christ is incomprehensible, the Holy Spirit is incomprehensible, and Heaven is incomprehensible, except as expressly revealed in the Scriptures.

As God is infinite or limitless, i.e., He knows no bounds and is measureless, so Heaven is infinite and measureless. There is no time there, for all is eternity. We might say that *time stands still* in the place with the presence of God. There is neither hurry nor deadlines to meet.

As God is immutable or unchangeable, so is Heaven. It is the one place that will never change, for it is perfection itself.

The pinnacle of God's creative power, *In the beginning God created the heavens and the earth,* was not the earth itself, not the heaven around the earth, nor the heaven beyond the heavens, but the third Heaven or place of God's abode. It is a place as incomprehensible as God Himself.

> *Thou, even Thou, art LORD alone; Thou hast made heaven, the heaven of heavens, with all their host, the earth, and all things that are therein, the seas, and all that is therein, and Thou preservest them all; and the host of heaven worshippeth Thee* (Nehemiah 9:6).

A.W. Tozer said the following of God, but it applies equally to Heaven.

> When we try to imagine what Heaven is like, we must of necessity use that-which-is-not-Heaven as the raw material for our minds to work on; hence whatever we visualize Heaven to be, it is not, for we have constructed our image out of that which is not Heaven
>
> Left to ourselves we tend to imagine Heaven in terms that we are familiar with—this earth and all its relationships. Christians need the feeling of security and continuity that comes from knowing what Heaven is like, and what

Heaven is like has come from paintings, songs, books, T.V., movies, preachers, teachers, and all the sublime ideas we have entertained.

The yearning to comprehend the incomprehensible arises from the image of Heaven in the nature of man. (A. W. Tozer, *The Knowledge of the Holy,* Faithful Life Publishers).

We believe Heaven to be what we imagine Heaven to be. And so, we have taken what we know from our sojourn on this earth, and transposed it into our concept of Heaven. Therefore, we say, "Heaven is, or must be...," because of what we have experienced here.

Because Heaven is generally incomprehensible to those on earth, we must rely on the revelation of Heaven as found in God's Word—the Bible. It is only in His Book that God takes what we do not know, and reveals the parts we can know and comprehend.

My desire is to help. This book is written to help comfort and encourage those that have placed their faith in the finished work of Jesus Christ on the Cross of Calvary, those who are themselves facing the journey from this life to eternal life in Heaven. This book will also give the lost (those without faith in Christ) insight into the process of death from God's viewpoint. At the end of this book, the unsure and the lost will find what is called *God's Plan of Salvation.* Please avail yourself of this biblical summary of what God requires for a lost person to become a saved person, for it is only the saved that are allowed to enter Heaven.

> *Jesus saith unto him, 'I Am the way,* [I Am] *the truth, and* [I Am] *the life: no man cometh unto the Father, but by Me'* (John 14:6).

Since my desire is to help, I can best help by carefully recording what the Bible says about Heaven, even when it conflicts with what we have thought or have been taught.

A couple reminders for those on the journey:

1.  The person who comes to Christ is made positionally dead (before God) to this world system. It is easier to physically die, if you are already dead! (See Romans chapter 6)

2.  The person who comes to Christ is made positionally dead to himself. Once again, it is easier to physically die, if you are already dead! (See Romans 12:1-2)

3.  Because you are now dead to this world and self, you have become a pilgrim, a stranger, and

a sojourner in regard to this world's system. You have already pulled up your earthly roots and are simply abiding (an active word) in Christ until He calls you home.

Still, my desire is to help. During the home going of my wife, I have given more than ample time to considering death. One area that the Lord has impressed upon me is the possibility that though born-again Christians are *ready* to meet the Lord, they are *not ready* to die. You see, in most cases, death is a process, as opposed to an instantaneous, uncontrollable event. And it is that process that God uses to bring many of His children to Heaven. It is not that God personally causes death in its many stages, but that He allows the divine process of death to work His will for His child's ultimate good. I personally cannot say what God's ultimate plan for your home-going is or is going to be, but these two things I do know.

> *Precious in the sight of the LORD is the death of His saints* (Psalm 116:15).
> *'For I know the thoughts that I think toward you' saith the LORD, 'thoughts of peace, and not of evil, to give you an expected end'* (Jeremiah 29:11).

The Bible says, some 189 times, that someone *died*. The Bible puts it thus in Exodus 2:23, *And it came to pass in process of time, that...died.*" The truth is that from the moment of conception, we all begin the journey that ends in death. In fact, life itself is a terminal disease.

> *And the time drew nigh that Israel* (Jacob) *must die* (Genesis 47:29).

> *What man is he that liveth, and shall not see death? shall he deliver his soul from the hand of the grave? Selah* (think on this) (Psalm 89:48).

> *Wherefore, as by one man* (Adam) *sin entered into the world, and death by sin* (missing God's standard); *and so death passed upon all men, for that all have sinned* (Romans 5:12).

Death is the general rule—the exception is the *catching away* at the Lord's return in the clouds (See 1 Thessalonians 4:13-18).

# Death

- There is the death of a child or infant (King David's child at 2 Samuel 12:13).

- There is the peaceful death of long years (Methuselah at Genesis 5:27).

- There is a journey through the valley of the shadow of death (Psalm 23:4).

- There is the powerlessness of man over death (Ecclesiastes 8:8).

- There is the *shadow of death* that follows every man from the cradle to the grave (Matthew 4:16).

- There is the violent familial death that sometimes rears its ugly head (Matthew 10:21).

- There is the familial death of retribution, mostly unheard of in today's modern society (Matthew 15:4).

- There is the death of sorrow, or of the broken heart (Matthew 26:38).

- There is a death that is the result of the wages of sin (Romans 6:23).

- There is a death in the flesh, but a quickening in the Spirit (1 Peter 3:18).

- There is a death that delivers another soul from the second death (James 5:20).

- There is a death that is full of life and love (1 John 3:14).

- There is a death that is sought because of circumstances (Revelation 9:6).

- There is a death that comes because of wrong life-style choices (Revelation 2:23).

- There is the death wherein the believer stays faithful to his/her profession and receives a crown of life (Revelation 2:10).

## The Blessedness of Death

*For this God is our God for ever and ever: He will be our guide even unto death...* (Psalm 48:14).

*A good name is better than precious ointment; and the day of death than the day of one's birth* (Ecclesiastes 7:1).

*Verily, verily, I* (Jesus) *say unto you, 'He that heareth My Word, and believeth on Him* (God) *that sent Me, hath everlasting life, and shall not come into condemnation; but is passed from death unto life'* (John 5:24).

*So when this corruptible* [human body] *shall have put on incorruption, and this mortal shall have put on immortality, then shall be brought to pass the saying that is written, 'Death is swallowed up in victory'* (1 Corinthians 15:54).

*That I may know Him* (Christ), *and the power of His resurrection, and the fellowship of His sufferings, being made conformable unto His death* (Philippians 3:10).

## The Conclusion of the Matter

*Casting all your care upon Him; for He careth for you.* (1 Peter 5:7)

*But as it is written, Eye hath not seen, nor ear heard, neither have entered into the heart of man, the things which God hath prepared for them that love Him. But God hath revealed them unto us by His* [Holy] *Spirit: for the Spirit searcheth all things, yea, the deep things of*

*God. For what man knoweth the things of a man, save the spirit of man which is in him? even so the things of God knoweth no man, but the Spirit of God. Now we have received, not the spirit of the world, but the Spirit which is of God; that we might know the things that are freely given to us of God. Which things also we speak, not in the words which man's wisdom teacheth, but which the Holy Ghost teacheth; comparing spiritual things with spiritual.* (1 Corinthians 2:9-13)

May God fill your heart with joy and peace as you are preparing for the most exciting journey of your life.

# Afraid? Of What?

To feel the spirit's glad release?
To pass from pain to perfect peace?
The strife and strain of life to cease?
Afraid—of that?

Afraid to see the Saviour's face?
To hear His welcome, and to trace,
The glory gleam from wounds of grace?
Afraid—of that?

A flash, a crash, a pierced heart:
Darkness, light, O Heaven's art!
A wound of His, a counterpart!
Afraid—of that?

To do by death what life could not—
Baptize with blood a stony plot,
Till souls shall blossom from the spot?
Afraid—of that?

## The letter from Heaven, written from where time is no more.

Dearest Greg:

I have arrived!

I remember the last few days in the hospital. I know that I could not express myself verbally, but I heard all that went on around me. I remember your prayers, your testimonies of love, and even the sound of your soft breathing through all those long nights. I remember the kindness of the nurses and doctors, and the voice they gave to the peace that permeated our room. I remember the sweet words of comfort from Pastor Jim and Suzanne. I remember the presence of Phil and Sharon, and their "just being there" to do whatever they could. I remember finding comfort in the knowledge of the prayers of family and friends. I remember our son and granddaughter being in the room for a time.

I remember all the hands that held mine—that oh so very human impulse—and you running that green "frog" over my aching muscles. I remember wanting to be faithful to the words you often heard me say, "God, may my testimony and witness remain intact in my last days." Mostly, I remember the faithfulness of Christ and His grace and mercy being sufficient for all my needs. Through Him I had peace. Through Him I had inexpressible joy. Even when the room was dark, my soul was full of the Light of life.

> *...I Am the Light of the world: he that followeth Me shall not walk in darkness, but shall have the Light of life* (John 8:12).

Well I remember coming to the point of struggling for that last breath, and you rushing to my side, calling for the nurse.

*...even we ourselves groan within ourselves, waiting for the adoption, to wit, the redemption of our body* (Romans 8:23).

I opened my eyes and looked at you. I couldn't speak and you would not have understood me if I did. You said, "I love you," and I was gone. At the moment of release from my body, I felt the weight of a thousand earthly cares lifted--and I ascended.

*If a man die, shall he live again? all the days of my appointed time will I wait, till my change come* (Job 4:14).

*Casting all your care upon Him; for He careth for you* (1 Peter 5:7).

*And deliver them who through fear of death were all their lifetime subject to bondage* (Hebrews 2:15).

I did not feel my soul and spirit leaving my body. I did not linger above my earthly temple waiting to be summoned upward. I had no time to look back at my earthly house slowly cooling on the hospital bed, nor did I want to.

> For we know that if our earthly house of this tabernacle were dissolved, we have a building of God, an house not made with hands, eternal in the heavens (2 Corinthians 5:1).

I do not remember the journey or the sensation of flight. It was instantaneous, and there was no sense of motion or travel. I was unaware of any angels guiding or accompanying me during my journey; no long tunnel with a light at the end; no beloved family members or friends standing on that far-flung shore awaiting my arrival. Many have spoken of seeing departed loved ones at the last, or hearing their voices calling ,'Come up hither,' but I neither heard nor saw those phenomenons.

> ...for the former things are passed away (Revelation 21:4).

At the last second of my earthly sojourn, I was lying on a hospital bed; at the first second of my eternal sojourn, I was prostrate before the Saviour.

> *For so an entrance shall be ministered unto you abundantly into the everlasting kingdom of our Lord and Saviour Jesus Christ* (2 Peter 1:11).

> *We are confident, I say, and willing rather to be absent from the body, and to be present with the Lord* (2 Corinthians 5:8).

My first heavenly recollection was of being bathed in the indescribable glory of God. It was light that in its clarity transcends description. My mind struggled to comprehend it; my eyes struggled to gain a foothold in that bright field of vision; and my heart raced with a mixture of fear and reverence. It was as a dream sequence, where nothing is focused, but all is a mist. I closed my eyes, fearful of the intensity of the light.

*Jesus saith unto her, 'Said I not unto thee, that, if thou wouldest believe, thou shouldest see the glory of God?'* (John 11:40).

*...and shewed me that great city, the holy Jerusalem, descending out of heaven from God, having the glory of God: and her light was like unto a stone most precious...* (Revelation 21:10).

My next memory was of lying prostrate before the throne of glory.

*And when I saw Him, I fell at His feet as dead* (Revelation 1:17a).

As I slowly opened my eyes, I realized that I was lying on a floor of transparent gold, clear as glass.

*...and the street of the city was pure gold, as it were transparent glass* (Revelation 21:21).

As my eyes adjusted, I could see that I was suspended over the vastness of the universe. It was then that I realized I was looking down at Creation from the top! I was overcome by the omniscience and omnipotence of my God, who created the vastness of space and the smallest particles that compose matter. I could see galaxies, stars, planets, and solar systems. I could even see the place of my worldly abode—earth. No, I had no ability to see or hear the activities of those left behind, for the universe only revealed the glory of God to my eyes.

*In the beginning God created...* (Genesis 1:1).

How long I laid there I cannot tell, but a soothing, settling male voice came to my ears. 'You have suffered many things on your journey, but I could bring you home by no other way. My sufferings, though to a lesser extent, became your suffering; but My grace to endure, became your grace to overcome.'

*For I reckon that the sufferings of this present time are not worthy to be compared with the glory which shall be revealed in us* (Romans 8:18).

*But ye are come unto mount Sion, and unto the city of the living God, the heavenly Jerusalem, and to an innumerable company of angels, To the general assembly and church of the firstborn, which are written in heaven, and to God the Judge of all, and to the spirits of just men made perfect, And to Jesus the mediator of the new covenant, and to the blood of sprinkling...* (Hebrews 12:22-24).

Deep in unfathomable mines,
With never-failing skill,
God treasures up His bright designs,
And works His gracious will.
(copied)

Finally, regaining my composure and lifting my head, I beheld the One standing by the throne. He was like a lamb which had been sacrificed.

*And I beheld, and, lo, in the midst of the throne and of the four beasts* (spirit beings), *and in the midst of the elders, stood a Lamb as it had been slain* (Revelation 5:6).

And I remembered the many Lord's Days that I had given scant thought to the suffering of my Saviour. I thought of the many opportunities that I had to partake of the Lord's Supper, when its reality did not move my heart. And I thought of the many yearly Passovers when His resurrection should have, but did not, fill my heart with joy unspeakable.

> *For as often as ye eat this bread, and drink this cup, ye do shew the Lord's death till He come* (1 Corinthians 11:26).

Looking closer, I saw the scars of where the nails had pierced His hands and His feet, and where the sword had pierced His side—for me!

> *Then saith He to Thomas, 'Reach hither thy finger, and behold My hands...'* (John 20:27).

Sitting on the throne, and beside the Lamb was God, Who was manifested in the Person of the Lord Jesus Christ. His countenance was like jasper, clear as crystal, and like a sardine (Sardis) stone, fiery ruby red, bespeaking purity, royalty, and redemption. He was dazzling to look upon. Out of the throne went forth lightnings, thunderings, and sounds. Before the throne burned the seven lamps, representing the

Holy Spirit of God, plus a great expanse of glass like crystal. Over the throne, like a diadem, was the rainbow of promise, its hues of brilliant color flashing with indescribable light. It was more than the mind could comprehend, yet it transfixed my eyes. To see God—what a wonder!

*Blessed are the pure in heart: for they shall see God* (Matthew 5:8).

*...behold, a throne was set in heaven, and One sat on the throne. And He that sat was to look upon like a jasper and a sardine stone: and there was a rainbow round about the throne, in sight like unto an emerald. And round about the throne were four and twenty seats: and upon the seats I saw four and twenty elders sitting, clothed in white raiment; and they had on their heads crowns of gold. And out of the throne proceeded lightnings and thunderings and voices: and there were seven lamps of fire burning before the throne, which are the seven Spirits of God. And before the throne there was a sea of glass like unto crystal: and in the midst of the throne, and round about the throne, were four beasts full of eyes before and behind. And the four beasts...rest not day and night,*

*saying, 'Holy, holy, holy, Lord God Almighty, which was, and is, and is to come'* (Revelation 4:2-8).

*God is a Spirit: and they that worship Him must worship Him in spirit and in Truth* (John 4:24).

*Who is the image of the invisible God, the Firstborn of every creature* (Colossians 1:15).

*For it pleased the Father that in Him should all fulness dwell* (Colossians 1:19).

And what a throne it was—glorious in its pure white presence, and majestic in its dimensions! Created out of single pearls were steps that drew the eye ever upward. The regal seat was supported by stays/supports with two lions on each side. Each step also had two lions on either side. All was overlaid with transparent gold signifying the deity of the Lion of the tribe of Judah. Here was enthroned the Christ, the Centerpiece in the atrium of the New Jerusalem, the holy city.

*And they saw the God of Israel: and there was under His feet as it were a paved work of a sapphire stone, and as it were the body* (essence) *of heaven in his* (its) *clearness* (purity) (Exodus 24:10).

46

*Moreover the king made a great throne of ivory, and overlaid it with the best gold. The throne had six steps, and the top of the throne was round behind: and there were stays on either side on the place of the seat, and two lions stood beside the stays. And twelve lions stood there on the one side and on the other upon the six steps: there was not the like made in any kingdom* (1 Kings 10:18-20).

*And I saw a great white throne, and Him that sat on it...* (Revelation 20:11).

As I gazed at the Christ, He had the appearance of the Ancient of Days, yet He looked ever-young. He was white and ruddy, clothed with a garment as white as the snow, and girded with a golden girdle. His hair was white like wool. His head was as if gold, with eyes as a flame of fire, yet He looked on me with eyes like doves' eyes, fitly set. His cheeks were like spices and His lips like lilies. His hands were like gold rings set with beryl. His legs were like marble, His feet like brass that was refined in a furnace. His voice was as the sound of many waters, but His words were most sweet. His overall countenance was like the sun. He was altogether lovely.

(This description is taken from Revelation 1, Daniel 7, and the Song of Solomon 5.)

*Thine eyes shall see the King in His beauty: they shall behold the land that is very far off* (Isaiah 33:17).

*Beloved, now are we the sons of God, and it doth not yet appear what we shall be: but we know that, when He shall appear, we shall be like Him; for we shall see Him as He is* (1 John 3:2).

And while I was transfixed by the sight of my Saviour, from around the throne I heard the sound of a multitude of people and spirit-beings (angels) praising God as if their very hearts would explode in adoration.

*And they sung a new song, saying, 'Thou art worthy to take the book, and to open the seals thereof: for Thou wast slain, and hast redeemed us to God by Thy blood out of every kindred, and tongue, and people, and nation'* (Revelation 5:9).

*After this I beheld, and, lo, a great multitude, which no man could number, of all nations, and kindreds, and people, and tongues, stood before the throne, and before the Lamb, clothed with white robes, and palms in their hands; And cried with a loud voice, saying, 'Salvation to our God which sitteth upon the throne, and unto the Lamb'* (Revelation 7:9-10).

*And after these things I heard a great voice of much people in Heaven, saying, 'Alleluia; Salvation and glory, and honour, and power, unto the Lord our God'* (Revelation 19:1).

As I joined in the chorus of praise, lifting my hands toward the throne, it was then that I noticed that I was clothed in white linen, pure and bright.

*He that overcometh, the same shall be clothed in white raiment...* (Revelation 3:5).

And though I was clothed, and had left my earthly body cooling on the hospital bed, I had the similitude of my earthly body. I was recognizable. I had shape, form, and function, but to what degree is yet to be determined. I have thoughts, will, and emotions, but they are all in perfect harmony with God's thoughts, will, and emotions. All are now based on heavenly realities, instead of earthly apprehensions. I have lost access to my own sub-conscious, which is the receptacle of all my sins—for sins have no place in Heaven.

> *There are also celestial* (heavenly) *bodies, and bodies terrestrial* (earthly): *but the glory of the celestial is one, and the glory of the terrestrial is another* (1 Corinthians 15:40).

> *For in this we groan, earnestly desiring to be clothed upon with our house which is from heaven: If so be that being clothed we shall not be found naked* (2 Corinthians 5:2-3).

> *Who shall change our vile body, that it may be fashioned like unto His glorious body* (Philippians 3:21).

I have all five of my earthly senses, but every one of them is perfected. There is a sense that my "heavenly" spirit-body had been released from the sin-cursed condition on earth and had been brought to a state of flawless completion.

> *And He that sat upon the throne said, 'Behold, I make all things new'* (Revelation 21:5).

I am aware that in the not too distant future, by which I am no longer limited, that Christ will cause my heavenly spirit-body to be reunited with my earthly physical body, which will have been changed and glorified.

> *So also is the resurrection of the dead. It is sown in corruption; it is raised in incorruption: it is sown in dishonour; it is raised in glory: it is sown in weakness; it is raised in power: it is sown a natural body; it is raised a spiritual body. There is a natural body, and there is a spiritual body* (I Corinthians 15:42-44).

> *In a moment, in the twinkling of an eye, at the last trump: for the trumpet shall sound, and the dead shall be raised incorruptible, and we shall be changed* (1 Corinthians 15:52).

> *Beloved, now are we the sons of God, and it doth not yet appear what we shall be: but we know that, when He shall appear, we shall be like Him; for we shall see Him as He is* (1 John 3:2).

On that triumphant day, my Lord will summon each of His heavenly saints. Then we shall descend into the clouds of the sky to be eternally united with our glorified bodies that have been raised from their last resting place. It will not matter how or where the earthly body has met its end, for the Creator and Maker of it shall and can reassemble it to make it fit for Heaven.

> For if we believe that Jesus died and rose again, even so them also which sleep in Jesus will God bring with Him. For the Lord Himself shall descend from heaven with a shout, with the voice of the archangel, and with the trump of God: and the dead in Christ shall rise first...to meet the Lord in the air: and so shall we ever be with the Lord (1 Thessalonians 4:14, 16, 17).

My earthly body was corrupted, finite, and mortal. While I dwelt in it on earth, I had no idea that I was imprisoned in a body unfit for Heaven. What freedom to exist without those shackles that bound me to the earth and its sin! Now I am truly free, and when I receive my glorified body, I will be truly complete. Complete and free; and complete in Him!

*For this corruptible must put on incorruption, and this mortal must put on immortality. So when this corruptible shall have put on incorruption, and this mortal shall have put on immortality, then shall be brought to pass the saying that is written, 'Death is swallowed up in victory.' O death, where is thy sting? O grave, where is thy victory? The sting of death is sin; and the strength of sin is the Law. But thanks be to God, which giveth us the victory through our Lord Jesus Christ* (1 Corinthians 15:53-57).

*Whereby are given unto us exceeding great and precious promises: that by these ye might be partakers of the divine nature...* (2 Peter 1:4).

What joy it is to hear the angels rejoice each time a sinner is brought to repentance and faith in the Lord Jesus Christ. The New Jerusalem seems to shake with each shout.

*Likewise, I say unto you, there is joy in the presence of the angels of God over one sinner that repenteth* (Luke 15:7, 10).

Greg, Do you remember how I loved silence and disliked the drum-beat of the world? Though our Lord's throne is surrounded and engulfed with innumerable saints and spirit beings (angels), all are praising the Lamb who was slain. What a sight to behold the assembled spirit-beings, invisible on earth, but each in his place and order. The Seraphs with their six wings chanting 'Holy, holy, holy.' The Cherubs, with their four wings attending to the Lamb of God. The Archangels, with their two wings ready to fly at the command of Christ. And the four orders of Angels—Thrones, Dominions, Principalities, and Powers—all waiting to do God's pleasure.

> *Bless the LORD, ye His angels, that excel in strength, that do His commandments, hearkening unto the voice of His word. Bless ye the LORD, all ye His hosts; ye ministers of His, that do His pleasure* (Psalms 103:20, 21).

> *And the four beasts had each of them six wings about him; and they were full of eyes within: and they rest not day and night, saying, 'Holy, holy, holy, Lord God Almighty, which was, and is, and is to come'* (Revelation 4:8).

And the praise from around the throne! It is not the sound of noise, but the peace of adoration. It is a settled sound, like the burble of a mountain brook that glorifies Christ, not with noise, but with the realization of being in God's presence. It is the spirit-beings repeating, 'Glory to the Lamb who was slain,' while the saints glorify the Lamb in song.

> *My soul longeth, yea, even fainteth for the courts of the LORD: my heart and my flesh crieth out for the living God... even thine altars, O LORD of Hosts, my King, and my God. Blessed are they that dwell in Thy house: they will be still praising Thee. 'Selah'* (Psalm 84:2-4).

> *Be still, and know that I Am God...* (Psalm 46:10).

> *And they sung as it were a new song before the throne...* (Revelation 14:3).

What must it be to possess it? A home so happy, a rest so glorious, a place so high, a bliss so exquisite and enduring. This glorious Lamb! This glorious throne! These glorious ones with their glorious crowns! This effulgence of gracious Godhead! These sinless splendours! These eternal consolations! These holy services! These smiles of favour beaming from the King! These never-withering palms! These every-shining robes! These ever-thrilling songs! These ever-flowing springs of never-failing life! These joy-speaking eyes which never weep, and singing lips which never thirst, and uplifted hands which never tire, and comfort from God from which sorrow and sighing forever flee away! O blessed contemplation!

(Joseph Seiss, The Apocalypse,<br>Lectures on the Book of Revelation)

My eyes were now turned upward from the glory of the throne to the enormity of the New Jerusalem. It is this city that will be the home of the New Testament redeemed throughout eternity.

> *But Jerusalem which is above is free, which is the mother of us all* (Galatians 4:26).

> *For he looked for a city which hath foundations, whose Builder and Maker is God* (Hebrews 11:10).

*But now they desire a better country, that is, an heavenly: wherefore God is not ashamed to be called their God: for He hath prepared for them a city* (Hebrews 11:16).

*But ye are come unto mount Sion, and unto the city of the living God, the heavenly Jerusalem.* (Hebrews 12:22).

*For here have we no continuing city, but we seek one to come* (Hebrews 13:14).

*Him that overcometh will I make a pillar in the temple of My God, and he shall go no more out: and I will write upon him the Name of My God, and the name of the city of My God, which is New Jerusalem, which cometh down out of heaven from My God...* (Revelation 3:12).

The New Jerusalem is four-square, a fifteen-hundred mile high, wide and deep city.

*And the city lieth foursquare, and the length is as large as the breadth: and he measured the city with the reed, twelve thousand furlongs. The length and the breadth and the height of it are equal.* (Revelation 21:16).

The throne of God sits in its central atrium. Leading from this center atrium are innumerable hallways flanked by rooms on either side.

*In My Father's house are many mansions* (rooms down the hall; abiding places)*: if it were not so, I would have told you. I go to prepare a place* (room) *for you* (John 14:2).

The wall surrounding the city is two hundred and sixteen feet thick, having in each side three gates, each gate a single, massive pearl. The wall is constructed of jasper, a precious stone of various hues. And positioned at each gate is an angel. And inscribed on each gate is the name of one of the twelve tribes of Israel.

*And the twelve gates were twelve pearls; every several gate was of one pearl...* (Revelation 21:21).

*...at the gates twelve angels: and names written thereon, which are the names of the twelve tribes of the children of Israel* (Revelation 21:12).

The wall is supported by twelve foundations or steps to enter into the twelve gates of pearl. Each of the foundation steps is inscribed with the name of one of Christ's apostles. Each of the twelve foundations/

steps is adorned with a different precious stone.

> And the wall of the city had twelve foundations, and in them the names of the twelve apostles of the Lamb (Revelation 21:14).

> And the foundations of the wall of the city were garnished with all manner of precious stones. The first foundation was jasper; the second, sapphire; the third, a chalcedony; the fourth, an emerald; the fifth, sardonyx; the sixth, sardius; the seventh, chrysolite; the eighth, beryl; the ninth, a topaz; the tenth, a chrysoprasus; the eleventh, a jacinth; the twelfth, an amethyst (Revelation 21:19-20).

At the twelve gates begins the street or plaza of transparent gold, which stretches some 1500 miles long and wide. At its center point is the atrium and throne of the living God and the Lamb.

> ...and the street of the city was pure gold, as it were transparent glass (Revelation 21:21).

Greg, I remember your verbal portrait of this scene from one of your sermons: "On streets of gold, in a city of gold, to a throne of gold, to the One who received gifts of gold, amid the utensils of gold, we will see the One who is more precious than gold—the Lord Jesus Christ."

Out of this throne proceeds the crystal-clear, pure water of the river of life. This river follows its course as it moves throughout the golden plaza, dividing the plaza into streets. In the midst of the street and on each side of the river grow the trees of life. Their leaves are for the healing of the Gentile nations, while it continues to bear its twelve types of fruit every month. Eye has never viewed any river this pure, nor any tree this beautiful and productive.

> *And he shewed me a pure river of water of life, clear as crystal, proceeding out of the throne of God and of the Lamb. In the midst of the street of it, and on either side of the river, was there the tree of life, which bare twelve manner of fruits, and yielded her fruit every month: and the leaves of the tree were for the healing of the nations* (Revelation 21:1-2).

As I take in this glorious sight, I suddenly find myself in my place—the place Christ prepared just for me. I can't describe it, for it is mine alone, filled with reminders of what I did for Christ and what Christ did for me. It is as large or small as it needs to be. There is neither lack nor excess.

> *...I go to prepare a place* (room, space) *for you* (John 14:2).

> *Father, I will that they also, whom Thou hast given Me, be with Me where I Am; that they may behold My glory, which Thou hast given Me: for Thou lovedst Me before the foundation of the world* (John 17:24).

But the one aspect of the New Jerusalem that stands out is the total absence of darkness—not even a shadow! All is light and all is bathed in that Light that came to lighten the world, but men loved darkness. Here it is an indescribably pure, transcending light that permeates every corner and cupboard. It is a light that fills the soul, and all the space between the soul and God.

*Then spake Jesus again unto them, saying, 'I Am the Light of the world: he that followeth Me shall not walk in darkness, but shall have the Light of life'* (John 8:12).

*And the city had no need of the sun, neither of the moon, to shine in it: for the glory of God did lighten it, and the Lamb is the Light thereof* (Revelation 21:23).

I have not said much of the "former things" of your world, because they hold no sway over my eternal life in Heaven. On earth, I had many tears—here, only joy. On earth, death was a part of everyday living— here, death is no more. On earth, there was unending sorrow of one kind or another— here, there is not the thought of sorrow. On earth, I had many forms of pain, from physical to psychological—here, total release from my sin-cursed, earthly body.

*…in Thy presence is fulness of joy; at Thy right hand there are pleasures for evermore* (Psalm 16:11).

*There the wicked cease from troubling; and there the weary be at rest. There the prisoners rest together; they hear not the voice of the oppressor. The small and great are there; and the servant is free from his master* (Job 3:17-19).

*For our light affliction, which is but for a moment, worketh for us a far more exceeding* [and] *eternal weight of glory* (2 Corinthians 4:17).

*And God shall wipe away all tears from their eyes; and there shall be no more death, neither sorrow, nor crying, neither shall there be any more pain: for the former things are passed away* (Revelation 21:4).

As to my former relationship with people on earth, I have none. I no longer have a past, only an eternal present. I am unable and uninterested in viewing events that are even now exercising their influence over you. I have no ability to "see" what is happening on earth. Neither do I have the desire or ability to return to your earthly place of sin and sorrow. I have no ability to "bring back" the past, for my present so fills my being that the past has no place in me.

*...for the former things are passed away* (Revelation 21:4).

The only touchstone I have with earth is when a person comes to faith in Christ and Heaven rejoices.

*I say unto you, that likewise joy shall be in heaven over one sinner that repenteth* (Luke 15:7).

I no longer operate under the confines of my earthly intellect, emotions, and will. These are gone, perhaps only to be resurrected in my glorified body when I stand at the judgment seat of Christ. All these matters of the earthly head have been replaced with matters of the heavenly heart. I now have the mind of Christ, the will of the Father, and the "emotions" of the Holy Spirit. The spiritual battles of the past have been replaced by the spiritual victory of the present.

*And this is the will of Him that sent Me, that everyone which seeth the Son, and believeth on Him, may have everlasting life: and I will raise him up at the last day* (John 6:40).

*...But we have the mind of Christ* (1 Corinthians 2:16).

*...but the Spirit itself maketh intercession for us with groanings which cannot be uttered* (Romans 8:26).

My sin-laden, sub-conscience memory-bank is no more, until my glorified body and heavenly soul are reunited to stand at the Judgment Seat of Christ. Then, when my Saviour searches my soul, He will say, "Well?" and I will reply, "Done. It was even as You said."

> For we must all appear before the judgment seat of Christ; that every one may receive the things done in his body, according to that he hath done, whether it be good or bad (2 Corinthians 5:10).

> Come, see a Man, which told me all things that ever I did: is not this the Christ? (John 4:29).

> And now, little children, abide in Him; that, when He shall appear, we may have confidence, and not be ashamed before Him at His coming (1 John 2:28).

Even my thoughts of you are gone—I know how hard that is for you to accept. I simply am not interested in the things of your heart, or the things of the earth that hold such sway over your body. I have been set free, never again to be held in bondage to the circumstances of human existence. Even our fifty years of earthly marriage holds no place in my present reality. I did marry you, but we are married no more. I did humanly love you, but I love you no more. I did cherish our moments together, but I cherish them no more. Your love, thoughts, and expectations are no longer mine, for my present love and thoughts are only and always of Christ.

> *For in the resurrection they neither marry, nor are given in marriage, but are as the angels of God in heaven* (Matthew 22:29-30).

> *And Jesus answering said unto them, 'The children of this world marry, and are given in marriage: but they which shall be accounted worthy to obtain that world, and the resurrection from the dead, neither marry, nor are given in marriage: Neither can they die any more: for they are equal unto the angels; and are the children of God, being the children of the resurrection'* (Luke 20:34-36).

> *For the woman which hath an husband is bound by the law to her husband so long as he liveth; but if the husband be dead, she is loosed from the law of her husband* (Romans 7:2).

*For we brought nothing into this world, and it is certain we can carry nothing out* (1 Timothy 6:7).

There God, our King and Portion,
In fullness of His grace,
We then shall see forever,
And worship face to face.
(copied)

I know you are curious about the relationship that believers have with family members in Heaven. When I first saw our Down's Syndrome son, we did not hug, we did not cry, but we both knew the bond that we once shared. I was no longer his mother and he was no longer my son, but we rejoiced together in what Christ had done for us, and for the privilege to glorify Him forever.  In the same way, I saw my mother, your sister, and your aunt. We also rejoiced over our eternal security in Christ.

On earth, I interacted with many others, some good and some not so good, but I did not know the purpose behind it. But in Heaven, though I no longer have the relationships, I know God's perfect purpose and plan in each of those earthly associations.

I have also had contact with those that Christ graciously allowed me to have a part in their salvation. Greg, you are one of those—I joyously await your arrival.

Is it any wonder that Heaven is a place of continuous joy and rejoicing?

> And we know that all things work together for good to them that love God, to them who are the called according to His purpose (Romans 8:28).

> For now we see through a glass, darkly; but then face to face: now I know in part; but then shall I know even as also I am known (1 Corinthians 13:12).

What do I do in Heaven, you may wonder? There is no weariness here, so my activity is continuous. There is no night here, so my activity is uninterrupted. There is no boredom here, so my life is full and exciting.

There is the continual wonder of the throne and the Lord Jesus Christ who resides thereupon. There is the opportunity to sit at Christ's feet, as He opens the Scriptures. There is the blessing of gazing on the face of God in Jesus Christ. There are the song "services" where we express our adoration to the Lamb who was slain. There is the rest and peace of life without the Curse. There is the indescribable beauty of the city of gold and its many fascinations. There is the continual inquiry by the spirit-beings into the doctrine of salvation. There is the sacred opportunity of serving Christ in a priestly capacity. And there is much more. My life is now full of meaning and that for eternity.

> *And they sing the song of Moses the servant of God, and the song of the Lamb, saying, 'Great and marvellous are Thy works, Lord God Almighty; just and true are Thy ways, Thou King of saints'* (Revelation 15:3).

> *Heaven and earth shall pass away, but My words shall not pass away* (Matthew 24:35).

*To the intent that now unto the principalities and powers* (orders of angels) *in heavenly places might be known by the church the manifold wisdom of God* (Ephesians 3:10).

*Searching what, or what manner of time the Spirit of Christ which was in them did signify, when it testified beforehand the sufferings of Christ, and the glory that should follow...which things the angels desire to look into* (1 Peter 1:11-12).

*And there shall be no more curse: but the throne of God and of the Lamb shall be in it; and His servants shall serve Him: And they shall see His face; and His Name shall be in their foreheads* (Revelation 22:3-4).

*By Him therefore let us offer the sacrifice of praise to God continually, that is, the fruit of our lips giving thanks to His Name* (Hebrews 13:15).

Do I eat, drink, and sleep? Not of necessity because I am in the spirit, and have no need of those earthly requirements. And it should be the same when I am reunited with my glorified body. But my Saviour, in His glorified body, ate in the presence of His disciples. So, even though I have no need of food or drink, I have access to both from the trees of life and from the crystal river. This is not to fulfill a physical need, like on earth, but to fulfill a spiritual need of remembering that God is the God of all provision. And, oh, the exquisiteness of His provision!

> *As soon then as they were come to land, they saw a fire of coals there, and fish laid thereon, and bread. Jesus saith unto them, 'Come and dine'... Jesus then cometh, and taketh bread, and giveth them, and fish likewise* (John 21:9, 12, 13).

> *They shall hunger no more, neither thirst any more; neither shall the sun light on them, nor any heat. For the Lamb which is in the midst of the throne shall feed them, and shall lead them unto living fountains of waters...* (Revelation 7:16-17).

> *And he shewed me a pure river of water of life, clear as crystal, proceeding out of the throne of God and of the Lamb. In the midst of the street of it, and on either side of the river, was there the tree of life, which bare twelve manner of fruits, and yielded her fruit every month: and the leaves of the tree were for the healing of the nations* (Revelation 22:1-2).

*To him that overcometh will I give to eat of the tree of life, which is in the midst of the paradise of God* (Revelation 2:7).

*To him that overcometh will I give to eat of the hidden manna...* (Revelation 2:17).

Oh, Greg, there is so much more. And though I can comprehend all things, I do not have the ability to put into human words the wonders of the Person or the place of my abode. It is beyond human comprehension, but it is not beyond the saint's heavenly pleasure.

How I look forward to the day of your arrival. Not because you are more important than the meanest of saints, but because we found Christ and shared Christ together for all those years. How wonderful it will be to see the light of the countenance of Christ in your face as He lightens mine.

*Thou wilt shew me the path of life: in Thy presence is fulness of joy; at Thy right hand there are pleasures for evermore* (Psalm 16:11).

*They shall be abundantly satisfied with the fatness of Thy house; and Thou shalt make them drink of the river of Thy pleasures* (Psalm 36:8).

*He that overcometh shall inherit all things; and I will be his God, and he shall be My son* (Revelation 21:7).

*That in the ages to come He might shew the exceeding riches of His grace in His kindness toward us through Christ Jesus* (Ephesians 2:7).

And yes, I still have future things to look forward to. First, and foremost, is the catching away of the dead and living saints in Christ from off of the earth. At that moment my living soul and my resurrected body will be reunited into one glorified body like as Christ has.

*As for me, I will behold Thy face in righteousness: I shall be satisfied, when I awake, with Thy likeness* (Psalm 17:15).

*Knowing that He which raised up the Lord Jesus shall raise up us also by Jesus, and shall present us with you* (2 Corinthians 4:14).

*For if* (since) *we believe that Jesus died and rose again, even so them also which sleep in Jesus will God bring with*

*Him. For this we say unto you by the word of the Lord, that we which are alive and remain unto the coming of the Lord shall not prevent* (precede) *them which are asleep. For the Lord Himself shall descend from heaven with a shout, with the voice of the archangel, and with the trump of God: and the dead in Christ shall rise first: then we which are alive and remain shall be caught up together with them in the clouds, to meet the Lord in the air: and so shall we ever be with the Lord* (1 Thessalonians 4:4-17).

Second will be the Judgment (Bema) Seat of Christ, where every born-again believer will see his/her life for what it really was in the sight of God. This will be the final step in our salvation and sanctification.

*For we must all appear before the judgment seat of Christ; that every one may receive the things done in his body, according to that he hath done, whether it be good or bad* (2 Corinthians 5:10).

*For other foundation can no man lay than that is laid, which is Jesus Christ. Now if any man build upon this Foundation gold, silver, precious stones, wood, hay, stubble; every man's work shall be made manifest: for the day* [of judgment] *shall declare it, because it shall be revealed by fire; and the fire shall try every man's work of what sort it is. If any man's work abide which he hath built thereupon, he shall receive a reward. If any man's work shall be burned, he shall suffer loss: but he himself shall be saved; yet so as by fire* (1 Corinthians 3:11-15).

Third will be the awesome privilege to sit with the Lord Jesus Christ upon His throne.

*To him that overcometh will I grant to sit with Me in My throne, even as I also overcame, and am set down with My Father in His throne* (Revelation 3:21).

Fourth will be the marriage of the Lamb to His bride. This will be the bringing together, into one body, the individual bodies of Christ (His churches), which down through the centuries have suffered persecution for His Name's sake. This heavenly body will become the bride of Christ—spotless and pure—honored and revered for its labor of love.

Written to the church at Corinth—*For I am jealous over you with godly jealousy: for I have espoused you to one husband, that I may present you as a chaste virgin to Christ* (2 Corinthians 11:2).

Written to the church at Ephesus—*There is one body, and one Spirit, even as ye are called in one hope of your calling; One Lord, one faith, one baptism* (Ephesians 4:4-5).

*That He might present it to Himself a glorious church, not having spot, or wrinkle, or any such thing; but that it should be holy and without blemish* (Ephesians 5:27).

*Let us be glad and rejoice, and give honour to Him: for the marriage of the Lamb is come, and his wife hath made herself ready. And to her was granted that she should be arrayed in fine linen, clean and white: for the fine linen is the righteousness of saints* (Revelation 19:7-8).

Fifth will be the marriage supper of the Lamb, which will take place after the wedding, both in the New Jerusalem and on earth during the millennial (1,000 year) reign of Jesus Christ.

*Again, He sent forth other servants, saying, 'Tell them which are bidden, Behold, I have prepared My dinner: My oxen and My fatlings are killed, and all things are ready: come unto the marriage'* (Matthew 22:4).

*Let us be glad and rejoice, and give honour to Him: for the marriage of the Lamb is come, and His wife hath made herself ready* (Revelation 19:7).

*And he saith unto me, 'Write, Blessed are they which are called unto the marriage supper of the Lamb'. And he saith unto me, 'These are the true sayings of God'* (Revelation 19:9).

Sixth will be the privilege of ruling and reigning with Jesus Christ during Christ's 1000 year kingdom on earth.

*And hath made us kings and priests unto God and His Father* (Revelation 1:6).

*And he that overcometh, and keepeth My works unto the end, to him will I give power over the [Gentile] nations* (Revelation 2:26 ).

*And hast made us unto our God kings and priests: and we shall reign on the earth* (Revelation 5:10).

Greg, how happy I am, how safe I feel, and how awe-inspiring are the works of God. On earth, I could not comprehend the glories of Heaven, and in Heaven I cannot comprehend the sorrows of earth.

*And I give unto them eternal life...* (John 10:28).

*But as it is written, Eye hath not seen, nor ear heard, neither have entered into the heart of man, the things which God hath prepared for them that love Him* (1 Corinthians 2:9).

*To an inheritance incorruptible, and undefiled, and that fadeth not away, reserved in heaven for you* (1 Peter 1:4).

But you are still there and I am here. You still have service for Christ to do, and needful sanctification to occur to prepare you for Heaven. Though God requires good works of you while on earth, it is the spiritual preparation that will count for eternity up here. So use the time wisely that God has granted you, and when He calls you home you will have crowns to present to Christ.

*And every man that striveth for the mastery is temperate in all things. Now they do it to obtain a corruptible crown; but we an incorruptible* (1 Corinthians 9:25).

*Therefore, my brethren dearly beloved and longed for, my joy and crown, so stand fast in the Lord, my dearly beloved* (Philippians 4:1).

*For what is our hope, or joy, or crown of rejoicing? Are not even ye in the presence of our Lord Jesus Christ at His coming?* (1 Thessalonians 2:19).

*Henceforth there is laid up for me a crown of righteousness, which the Lord, the righteous Judge, shall give me at that day: and not to me only, but unto all them also that love His appearing* (2 Timothy 4:8).

*I beseech you therefore, brethren, by the mercies of God, that ye present your bodies a living sacrifice, holy, acceptable unto God, which is your reasonable service. And be not conformed to this world: but be ye transformed by the renewing of your mind, that ye may prove what is that good, and acceptable, and perfect, will of God* (Romans 12:1-2).

*Blessed is the man that endureth temptation: for when he is tried, he shall receive the crown of life, which the Lord hath promised to them that love Him* (James 1:12).

*And when the chief Shepherd shall appear, ye shall receive a crown of glory that fadeth not away* (1 Peter 5:4).

*Fear none of those things which thou shalt suffer: behold, the devil shall cast some of you into prison, that ye may be tried; and ye shall have tribulation ten days: be thou faithful unto death, and I will give thee a crown of life* (Revelation 2:10).

*Behold, I come quickly: hold that fast which thou hast, that no man take thy crown* (Revelation 3:11).

Greg, Christ is preparing a place for you, just as He has for me. I know not the path that you will walk, but I know it is a narrow way that leads to eternal life. As you once said, "The throes of death are the last-ditch effort of the sin-nature to hold on to its victim." But as I always said, "This too shall pass."

I am no longer your help-meet. I am no longer with you to encourage your steps, but the Word of God is a lamp unto your feet and a light for your path. Follow hard after your high calling in Christ Jesus, and I will see you soon at the eternal Throne.

Eternally with Christ,

Barbara

*Fear none of those things*
*which thou shalt suffer...*
*be thou faithful unto death,*
*and I will give thee a crown of life.*
**(Revelation 2:10)**

# The Heavenly Page

Dear Friend,

Perhaps you have picked up this volume out of curiosity, or perhaps you have an interest in the contents of this book. We welcome you to its pages, no matter the circumstances of your being here! You will find that this book is a treasure-trove of insights into Heaven, focusing on the Lord Jesus Christ. Why is that important, you might ask? Well, because the decision you make concerning the Lord Jesus Christ will determine where you will spend eternity.

How can you actually know that your future is secure? Because God has provided the Bible that you might have the answers and the solution to the age-old question, "Where will I go when I die?" God's Word, the Bible, reveals how trusting Jesus Christ as your Saviour will gain for you eternal life at your death, and abundant life in Christ until then. Now, isn't that what you *really* want? Let me explain how you can have eternal life in Heaven.

## What is the problem?

God cannot allow sin into Heaven, and you are a sinner by nature and by choice. When Adam, the first man, disobeyed God in the Garden of Eden, Adam's sin brought death (eternal separation from God) upon all mankind. So as a sinner, you are already separated from God eternally.

The Bible says it best, *For all have sinned* (missed God's standard) *and come short of the glory of God* (Romans 3:23).

## What is the payment?

The pleasures of sin (disobedience toward God) come at a price. The Bible says it best, *For the wages* (what you earn) *of sin is death* (eternal separation from God) (Romans 6:23a). All sin must be punished or God would not be a just God. And because God is an eternal Person, it would take an eternity for you to pay for your own sins. And that is exactly what Hell is, a place where you spend eternity paying for your sins.

## What is the privilege?

A free gift! Because God knew that man would fall into sin, from the dawn of creation God made a way for a man or woman to be reconciled to Himself. This simply means that God made a way for Himself and man to be brought back into a close relationship. This is accomplished, not by something you do, but by what Jesus Christ has already done for you on the cross of Calvary.

The Bible says it best, *But the* [free] *gift of God is eternal life through Jesus Christ our Lord* (Romans 6:23b).

## What is the proper perspective?

You are a sinner. Although God is angry with the wicked every day, He also proved His love toward sinners by coming to earth. He took on human flesh, living some 33 years as a Man, yet at the same time remaining fully God. He voluntarily submitted to death on the Cross to satisfy the just wrath of a holy God. Only a sinless Man could die for sinful men, and only an eternal Person could satisfy the wrath of an eternal God toward sinners. Jesus Christ was both fully Man and God, therefore He could fulfill every requirement of the holy Judge.

The Bible says it best, *But God commendeth* (proves) *His love toward us* (sinners), *in that, while we were yet sinners, Christ died for us* (Romans 5:8).

## What is the proof?

Jesus was crucified (nailed to a cross) by sinners. Jesus forgave those sinners. God poured out His wrath toward sin upon Jesus Christ for three long hours and the earth was darkened! Jesus, by His own authority, gave up the spirit of His life and died. His body was sealed in a tomb that was guarded by soldiers. On the third day Jesus, by His own authority, rose from the dead and rose from the tomb. He was seen by the apostles, by the women who ministered to Him, by 120 church members, and by at least 500 other people.

The Bible says it best, *For I delivered unto you first of all that which I also received, how that Christ died for our sins according to the scriptures; and that He was buried, and that He rose again the third day according to the scriptures: and that He was seen...* (1 Corinthians 15:3-5).

## What is the possible prerogative?

You can reject God's plan and work your own plan, but you will not be happy with where you will spend eternity. Or you can bow your heart and knee to the Lord Jesus Christ, trusting Him for forgiveness of sin and an eternal home in Heaven.

The Bible says it best, *That if thou shalt confess* (agree) *with thy mouth the Lord Jesus* (that Jesus is God), *and shalt believe in thine heart* (inner man) *that God hath raised Him from the dead, thou shalt be saved* (delivered from the penalty of your sins). *For whosoever* (that's you) *shall call upon the name of the Lord shall be saved* (Romans 10:9, 13).

## Believe—Repent—Pray,

"God, be merciful to me a sinner who believes in my heart that Jesus Christ paid the full payment of my sin-debt; that He fully satisfied the wrath of God on my behalf through His shed blood; and that God raised Him from the dead, fully satisfied with His sacrifice. I now repent of my sins and trust Jesus Christ's death alone for my salvation. In Jesus' name I pray, amen." (See John 3:16).

### *And so you have entered into eternal life!*

# I Could See God Tonight

I could see God tonight,
If my heart were right.
If all the rubbish of my soul
Were cleared away,
My being whole,
My breast would thrill in glad surprise,
At all the wonder in my eyes—tonight!
If only my dull heart were right.

If, you, O heart were right,
I could see God tonight.
And in the radiance of His face,
I'd flame with light
And fill this place with glory,
And the world would know how
God meets man down here below—tonight!
If you, O heart of mine, were right!

(copied)

**Note:** The two poems that follow are from a collection of Civil War literature which spoke to my heart during and after the home-going of my wife, Maybe, they will speak to your heart also.

# For My Loved One in the Grave

Oh are the heavens clear, ye say?
Oh is the air still sweet?
Oh is there joy yet in the day,
And life yet in the street?

I thought the sky in tears would break,
I thought the winds would rave,
I thought that every heart would ache
For my loved one in the grave.

Oh mankind has a cruel heart
To smile when mine's so sore!
Oh deeper stings the cruel smart
Than e'en it did before!

How can the merry earth go dance,
And all the banners wave,
The children shout, the horses prance,—
And my loved one's in the grave?

Charles Goodrich Whiting

# A Quiet House

My house is quiet now—so still!
All day I hear the ticking clock;
The hours are numbered; clear and shrill
Outside the robin's chirp and trill:
My house is quiet now—so still!

But silence breaks my heart. I wait,
And waiting yearn for call or knock,
To hear the creaking of the gate
And footsteps coming, soon or late:
The silence breaks my heart. I wait.

All through the empty house I go,
From hall to hall, from room to room;
The heavy shadows spread and grow,
The started echoes mock me so,
As through the empty house I go.

Ah, silent house! If I could hear
Sweet noises in the tranquil gloom,
The joyous tumult, loud and near,
That vexed me many a happy year—
Ah, silent house, if I could hear!

Ah, lonely house! If once, once more,
My longing eyes might see the stain
Of your wet footprints on the floor—
Your sweet, smiling face at the door—
Ah, blessed Heaven, but once, once more!

My house and home are very still.
I watch the sunshine and the rain:
The years go on . . . Perhaps Death will
Life's broken promises fulfil.
My house, my home, my heart, are still!

Mary Ainge De Vese

# Index of Scripture References

# ABOUT THE AUTHOR

Gregory Darst was saved and baptized in an independent Baptist church in 1976 at age 34. He was called to preach in October of 1980. Entering Baptist University of America in Atlanta, Georgia in 1981, Greg completed the requirements for a B.A. in theology and one year of postgraduate work, graduating with honors in 1984.

Since graduation, Brother Darst has pastored two independent Baptist churches before entering his present writing, teaching, and itinerant preaching ministry. God has also allowed him the opportunity to preach and teach His Word during seventeen overseas trips, plus various conferences and revivals in the USA.

In his teaching ministry, Brother Darst has taught verse by verse through Matthew (13 years); verse by verse through Revelation (5 years); and verse by verse through the Song of Solomon (2 years) all based on a unique Christ-centered Sunday school teaching method that God allowed him to develop.

In his writing ministry, Brother Darst has published two books; 1) *The Revelation of Jesus Christ in the Old Testament*, which is a guide to every Old Testament mention of Jesus Christ, and 2) *The Letter from Heaven: It's Not What You've Imagined*, a Scripture-based letter from his wife in Heaven. He has also completed a unique Bible commentary on the Song of Solomon (*The Revelation of Jesus Christ in the Song of Solomon*), which has yet to be published. Brother Darst was also a frequent contributor of articles to *The Pillar* magazine, plus the author of many booklets on Bible subjects.

A fellow Baptist pastor has said of him:

*He is a man with a special vision that dominates his entire life and ministry. That vision is to magnify the Name and Person of Jesus Christ, through his teaching, preaching and writing. All of us, of course, say that. But he is obsessed with it. I must admit, I have found it contagious. His preaching style is typically expository, and always with the express purpose of setting forth the glories of our Lord — "that in all things He might have the preeminence." This message is truly needed to encourage and unify God's people around Christ and His truth.*

Brother Darst and his wife Barbara had been married for 50 years. Barb went home to her Lord in April of 2016. Their oldest son, Garrick, was a pleasant, well-mannered Down's Syndrome child, who went home to his Lord in October of 2008. Their second son, Geoffrey, graduated from Bob Jones University, Greenville, SC, with a major in business and a minor in youth ministries. Brother Darst has four grandchildren.

For additional copies of this
book please order from:

**Faithful Life Publishers**
3335 Galaxy Way
North Fort Myers, FL 33903

www.FaithfulLifePublishers.com
(888) 720.0950

info@FLPublishers.com

or www.Amazon.com

For comments, questions, salvation decisions
or interactions of any kind, please contact:

G. Albert Darst

Web site: www.seekingchrist.net

Email: info@seekingchrist.net

CPSIA information can be obtained
at www.ICGtesting.com
Printed in the USA
FFOW03n0153260817
39135FF